I0190493

Espresso
FOR YOUR
GOALS™

*A Concentrated Energy
Boost for High Achievers
Who Know the Secret to
the Law Of Attraction*

LES GOODRICH

Espresso For Your Goals
A Concentrated Energy Boost For High Achievers
Who Know The Secret To The Law Of Attraction

Copyright © 2013 by Leslie Ernest Goodrich.
All rights reserved.

The contents of this book may not be
copied or reproduced without the prior
written permission of the author:
Goodrich, Leslie E. (12-31-2013).

The phrase: [Espresso For Your Goals]
is a trademark of, and is wholly owned by
Leslie Ernest Goodrich. 12-31-2013.

Published by DV8now Publishing
Vero Beach, FL
www.dv8now.com

Table of Contents

Introduction

Greetings! Thank you so much for buying my book. I can only imagine the journey that has led you here so let me first say welcome. I hope this concise little book is exactly what you have been looking for and with it you will find new energy for your goals and move ahead quickly to your highest benefit. This is an integrated system of highly effective tools to help established goal setters push beyond Law of Attraction basics and entry-level goal setting.

This book exists to inspire, motivate and facilitate the accomplishment of your top goals and visions, by building certainty with actions and results. It is intended for those who already perform at good or excellent levels, and are ready to accomplish something big, but are too responsible to take massive action without certainty. This is a simple but powerful system designed to help you generate that certainty so you can move ahead to whatever profound dreams you aspire to.

You may be familiar with some of the tools here and some may be completely new to you, but this is a powerful integration of process that has been refined for high achievers.

The remainder of the introduction consists of three sections: a short story that illustrates the most effective types of tools, the need for this book and the solutions it provides, and an overview of the contents.

A Story About the Most Effective Tools

A friend of mine is a highly skilled carpenter. He can build the most amazing creations from wood such as highly polished and perfectly seamless furniture, cabinetry, fine wood furnishings and detailed trim. He has a workshop of the most elaborate and sophisticated woodworking tools available.

One afternoon I was watching him work and I remarked that his collection of high-tech tools must make his job easier. He agreed, but he then asked me if I knew the most important tool in a carpenter's toolbox.

"What's that?" I asked. "A Pencil," he replied.

Indeed. None of his expensive tools could create anything without a clear plan, correct measurements and accurate markings. In fact, for the carpenter it is the simplest tools (pencil, hammer, screwdriver, square, level) that are used the most often and which remain for years for one reason: they work.

For high achieving goal setters and students of the Law of Attraction it's the same. The simple tools work. Traditionally our tools are clear goals, affirmations, visualization, inspired ideas and obvious tasks. In the chapters that follow I will define and present the *Espresso for Your Goals* system to combine the tools of achievement with concentrated alignment. And just like espresso, or my carpenter friend's pencil, this system is simple but powerful and effective.

The Need for This Book

This work arose when I clearly identified the need for a new paradigm in the world of motivational media. What happened was this.

I began to grow and evolve personally and professionally and much of that was thanks to my motivational heroes: Tony Robins, Les Brown, Zig Ziglar, Jack Canfield, John Assaraf, Mike Dooley and the ideas, tools and processes I learned from them and many others. I had reached a certain level of success—my house was paid for, my car was paid in full, I had absolutely no credit card debt, I had a successful newspaper column and a coveted corporate management position with a Fortune 500 company. I was making more money than I needed and my net worth was a solid six figures and rising. I was healthy, fit, grateful, happy with my family and friends, living a fun, active lifestyle but still striving to get to that next level that I knew I could achieve.

So I continued to seek out higher-level motivational content and then **I hit a wall.** The wall was that every time I watched a motivational speaker, read a motivational book, or listened to an audio or video presentation online, my vibration would invariably be dragged down when the presenter would begin to point out all of the problems of ineffective performers. You know the phrases they use!

"The problem is that most people_____",

"People always dwell on what they don't want because_____",

or the dreaded, *"You never achieve your goals because_____".*

So I thought, *wait a minute! Stop!* The time for motivational life coaches and writers to move beyond addressing their audiences as if they were all ineffective newbies is *now!*

Now I am not saying that the leaders I mentioned before specifically or only do this. I know that Tony Robins fills stadiums with high achievers. Les Brown speaks to the most successful people in the world. All I am saying is that *overall*, the motivational community *falls back on* illustrating *contrast* as a comfort zone in their public speaking and writing process. When I found myself having to navigate around those sections to keep my own thoughts positive, I knew there was a need for some **next-level motivational content**.

At the same time I knew that if I was going to move ahead, I had to grow beyond my own pieced-together collection of various deliberate creation procedures and develop **a concentrated set of aligned tools** that would cooperate in the direction of my goals and accomplish clear, undeniable results.

This book provides two solutions:

1. It spares established achievers the sob stories of poor performance and begins the material at a place beyond entry level, thereby providing much needed next-level motivational content.

2. It provides a simple yet potent system designed to leverage your goals, visions and actions and re-energize your accomplishment process with a concentrated set of aligned tools that delivers undisputed results.

Overview of the Sections That Follow

This book is organized in the order that you will use to create the initial system. Part of this process involves written goals (which you most likely already have). However, the *Espresso For Your Goals* system has methods for the wording and design of your Main Mission, Top 4 Goals, and Top 4 Visions that are the result of much refinement and research. As you work through the chapters ahead to design your personal *Espresso For Your Goals* system please stick to these overall methods at least for your initial run.

Once you have the process up and running you may (and should) fine-tune the components to serve you best. In fact, part of my *Espresso For Your Goals Seminar* involves a question and answer session where new and accomplished goal setters share experiences to improve this process.

So, yes, improve it for yourself when the time is right. But give it a month as it is presented to fully appreciate the system's interconnected nature, and to know what adjustments will better match your own style.

If you are beyond books that tell you what a goal is or what your problems are, and if you thrive on certainty built from results then let's get started. I hope you enjoy this journey as much as I have. Rock on!

CHAPTER 1

Main Mission

Your Main Mission is the overall reason for doing any of this. It is that one major life or career change that will make a significant difference in the quality of your current situation. Or (depending on your current level of accomplishment) it could also be a description of something you would like to maintain.

Think of it as the mission statement for your goal setting business plan. This section will define the qualities of the Main Mission, and describe the important position it holds in the system. At the end of this chapter, and before moving ahead, you will develop or refine your own Main Mission with clarity and certainty to form the basis of your highest accomplishments to follow.

Everyone will have different Main Missions and over time your own Main Mission will evolve, but there are two qualities that every Main Mission should have.

First your Main Mission should be **stated in the present and describe your ideal desired result.** Yes, this may sound familiar, but when I say *in the present*, I really mean it. Stretch beyond your casual ideas of present tense statements and **infuse your Main Mission with the crystal clear power of the current living** *now!*

Secondly, your Main Mission should be specific in terms of its intended outcome, but general in terms of its level of exact detail. For example, it would be better to say, "I am financially independent and free and earn an abundant living doing work I love," than "My novel, *Goal Wizard* is on the bestseller list and earning $1000 or more per week." In the first example, the intended outcome is specific: you want to be financially independent and free doing work you love. But the level of specific detail about exactly *how* is left to the Universe to deliver in the ways it knows best. The second affirmation about the specific novel and its sales might be a better Top 4 Goal (which we will get to later). But for the Main Mission leave that level of detail out of it.

Now much discussion has developed in the Goal Setting and Law of Attraction (LOA) communities around being specific versus going general. So, here is my understanding and viewpoint on the subject.

When defining something broad, like your Main Mission, going general (abundance, happiness, work you love, a mutually deserved relationship) does two very important things. First, and probably the most often used argument for going general with your goals, is that it leaves room for the Universe, or experience at large, to manifest your goal in the fastest, smoothest ways because you have not limited it with some specific detail. Yes, fine, I would agree. However, there is a second reason that I've grown to understand and this aspect is *extremely important*. Let me repeat that. *This second reason to go general with your broadest goals is of paramount importance with regard to your accomplishments.*

In addition to not limiting the Intelligent Universe as it conspires on your behalf along the road trip to your goals, going general with your Main Mission does not limit your *own* expectations and perceptions so that you will *recognize* those instances when the Universe gives you an opportunity to advance.

So yes, eliminate "exactly how in details" when you define your Main Mission. But when the Universe offers up an obvious *how*, pounce on it! Don't tinker with trying to design *how* and *exactly what* into your highest objectives, but when an *obvious how* presents itself—Pounce!

I will share with you my personal Main Mission, which I have refined over the last year or so. I believe that it illustrates the fundamentals of what you should be looking for, and I hope that it will be a clear example for you as you develop yours. So (just in the way of example) my Main Mission is as follows.

I am financially, professionally and
logistically independent and free <u>right now</u>!
I earn an abundant living being completely self-
employed. I decide if I am successful in my endeavors.
I work from wherever I choose to each day.

***

Here is your Chapter 1 assignment. Take some time to consider what your overall reason for setting and accomplishing goals is. What major life or career change will make a significant difference in the quality of your current situation? How would its ideal desired result look and feel in the absolute active now? How would you describe it to someone a year after you have been living it completely? Or if you are happy with your active situation, how can you polish and refine it to sparkle just a bit more? What would be even more ideal, or next level for you?

Then, write your Main Mission stated in the present and describing your ideal desired result. Infuse it with the crystal clear power of the current living now. Really include the words *now* or *right now* in the statement. Be passionate about the language you use and include serious words that have power for you. Make it general enough for maximum universal allowing and to free up your own perceptions and expectations.

Remember, you can always change, update, or refine it later (and you most likely will). So don't be too concerned about getting it exactly right. Write the best one you can. At this stage, *done is better than perfect.*

***

Your Main Mission will be the first component of your *Espresso For Your Goals* system. It will fit into the process and be referred to often so you should create your own physical version of it.

I like to write my Main Mission (and Top 4 Goals and Top 4 Visions) on 3x5 index cards. Some people may prefer a note on their computer, smartphone, or tablet. Personally, I like the tangible immediacy of index cards. A handwritten phrase carries its own physical power and 3x5 cards are the perfect size to keep things concise. Use what works best for you, but create your Main Mission in a readily available form and I will see you in Chapter two!

Chapter 2

Top 4 Goals

Now we will start to move into some of that specificity that we goal setters love so much. In this chapter you will create or refine your Top 4 Goals.

First, let's define my use of the terms *Goal* and *Vision*. For the purposes of this book and the *Espresso For Your Goals* system, I refer to **Goals** as those things you wish to **do** or **be**. I use the term **Vision** for those things you wish to **have** or **experience**. It is a distinction that I developed for my own journey of accomplishment and it has served me well. I will stick to these definitions throughout the book. *So in this system Goals are more personal performance, and Visions are more material experience.*

This section will define the aspects of our Top 4 Goals, and explain their importance as a second component in the system. At the end of this chapter you will create your own Top 4 Goals, or fit your existing goals into this format. Remember my suggestion to follow the system as designed at least for the first setup and use.

In much the same framework as your Main Mission, your Top 4 Goals should be stated as your ideal desired result and actively living in the present. They should focus on those things you wish to do or be. Think career, projects, relationship, fitness, health, and creative accomplishment.

Write your Top 4 Goals not only as your desired end result, but make them with certainty and in the most powerful present tense. Yes, add the words *now* or *right now* to them.

For example, below is one of my recent Top 4 Goals in two versions. The first is the way I created and used it (to much success I might add) before realizing the power of the infused passionate active living now. The second is a subtle revision that has made a remarkable difference in what I have achieved.

1. I am a published, professional, self-employed writer and speaker. (*See, nothing wrong with that. A textbook goal statement that worked just fine.*)

2. I am absolutely a published, professional, completely self-employed writer and speaker

<u>right now</u>! (*Do you see how different that feels? The difference is certainty and the conviction of this present moment.*)

Also, recognize how the second Top 4 Goal in my example above is more specific than my Main Mission, yet it is still general enough for unforeseen allowing.

Here is an important note on the popular subject of making your goals SMART, or Specific, Measurable, Achievable, Realistic and Time-Sensitive. Yes, these attributes are of high value for accomplishment. But in this system, we will reserve these SMART characteristics for the upcoming Action Section of our system. At this stage, the Goals and Visions are more about defining your Ideal Desired Result, and as such, the Time-Sensitive component is Now. Therefore, build your Top 4 Goals (and the upcoming Top 4 Visions) as describing the completed ideal desired result, so they will fuel the fire of the Law of Attraction by focusing your thoughts of what you desire, without the distractions of how and when. This is a new method, but a potent and effective one as you will see. Here is a powerful personal example of why that is so important.

As I was affirming and working toward this particular desire in my own Top 4 Goals (number two above) I got an email from John Assaraf. It was a course offered by Vic Johnson on writing and publishing eBooks that

John's *Praxis Now* organization was helping to promote. The first time I got that email I deleted it because I didn't think it applied to me. At the time my idea of being a writer was someone who writes and gets his work published as paper and ink books. I was sending out query letters and synopses to literary agents and the like. I had always thought of eBooks as being supplemental to an author's published printed book. (Often they are.)

But because my Top 4 Goal was to be a published, professional self-employed writer (and not a paper and ink novelist) the email caught my attention the second time around. I thought, *wait now. Writing, publishing and selling an eBook is being a published professional writer.*

When I looked into it I learned that many books are published as eBooks *first* and then become physical paper books. And some have long histories of success as eBooks alone. Because I had left some details about *how* out of my Top 4 Goal, I was open enough to recognize an opportunity I would have never thought of on my own. When I saw that chance though—when that obvious choice presented itself—I pounced on it (even if it took two tries by the Universe to get me to see it). Go general enough with your Top 4 Goals so you can do the same.

***

Here is your Chapter 2 assignment. Consider your goals. Narrow them down or increase them to the four most critical or important for you at this time. Write them with passion and enthusiasm in the present tense. Phrase them in certainty and include the words *now*, *right now*, or something else that convinces your heart of its immediacy.

Then record your Top 4 Goals in the same format as your Main Mission. If you used 3x5 notecards for the Main Mission, use them here as well. Again, whatever medium you choose, it should be readily and reliably available to you. You will refer to them often as a second component to your *Espresso For Your Goals* system.

Right now we are only listing the ingredients to this recipe. When we have each item ready, we will mix them all together and bake the concoction. I understand that some of this may sound like ground you have covered before, but judging it now would be like tasting plain flour to judge the flavor of the chocolate cake it will go into. I would also like to think that some of my insights are of value to you already. Come with me now as we explore deeper. Now is the time for us to press on together. On to Chapter Three!

CHAPTER 3

Top 4 Visions

Remember **Vision** refers to those things you wish to **have** or **experience**. Where Goals are more personal performance, Visions are more material experience.

This section will define the aspects of our Top 4 Visions. At the end of this chapter you will create your own Top 4 Visions, or fit your existing highest desires into this format. Once again they should be stated as your ideal desired result and actively living in the present. They should focus on those things you wish to **have** or **experience**. Think new car or home, a trip or vacation, a month in the Bahamas to work on your novel, an upgraded wardrobe, or a week riding your motorcycle on the Blueridge Parkway.

Now since we are getting into some detail here, it is worth noting that for such visions it will serve you to add certain caveats or open-endedness (such as the phrase "or better") so you don't restrict your allowing. Also be sure to include abundance and it's cousin, affordability as well. You want to be able to manifest a new car, let's say, without sacrificing a higher goal (such as financial independence). For instance, if I were adding a new car to my top four visions, I might phrase it like this:

I am thrilled to be driving my new BMW X5 (or something even better) right now! I can easily afford to own, drive and maintain it.

Now the less materialistic among us may have more virtuous Top 4 Visions, but from my viewpoint such desires are the decoration of life. But that's the beauty of deliberate creation; you can focus on what is important to you. Regardless of whether your Top 4 Visions include cars, road trips, helping others, or time with your family, infuse them with the powerful present, allow "even better" a place in their wording, and design them to develop as affordable and without compromise to your Top 4 Goals or Main Mission.

***

Here is your Chapter 3 assignment. Take the time now to write your Top 4 Visions. What Top 4 Visions would decorate your ideal life in the next year or so? Be detailed, but allow for even better. Infuse each with the dazzling active words *now* or *right now*. As before, record them in the same format that you used for your Main Mission and Top 4 Goals. Our ingredients are nearly all gathered. When you have your Top 4 Visions ready, join me in Chapter 4. Shake and Bake!

Pure Affirmations

Affirmations are the Law of Attraction tribe's bread and butter. The highest performing athletes, salespeople and entrepreneurs use them. In general, affirmations are thoughts that you deliberately focus on in order to bring about change, or achieve something you never have before.

In the *Espresso For Your Goals* system I have divided affirmations into two distinct types: Pure Affirmations and Refocus Affirmations. This chapter deals with Pure Affirmations, and the next chapter is focused on Refocus Affirmations.

Pure Affirmations are positive statements describing how you will feel and what you will experience when your ideal desired goals are achieved. *The purpose of a Pure*

Affirmation is to build belief in a possibility when you set out to accomplish something you have never done before. Overall, they are affirmations that point toward what you desire. They are also useful for affirming current aspects of gratitude.

Pure Affirmations are:

*Positive statements, set in the active living now, that describe your ideal desired result, or something you are grateful for.

*Relatively short phrases.

*To be read / glanced at quickly.

*Used to build neuro-pathways in the brain

*To program your subconscious mind.

*Not designed to "trick" or "convince" you that something is true if it isn't, but simply a tool to fuel the Law of Attraction by filling your mind with more of what you want.

You should have at least one Pure Affirmation for each of your Top 4 Goals and Top 4 Visions, but the quantity is not limited. I have about eighty on (you guessed it) 3x5 index cards. I quickly glance through them in about two minutes, once a day. The reason to glance at them quickly is so that your conscious mind does not have time to make a judgment about the statements. If one of your pure affirmations is *"I am so happy and grateful that I have $50,000. in my savings account,"* when you don't yet, you just want to glance at the card without entering into an internal debate about it. Read it fast, then before you can evaluate it, move on to the next card.

Remember, your subconscious mind has no filter. It records everything it perceives. This is why those of us who become aware of our power as deliberate creators tend to shy away from horror movies and negative news programs; who needs it? And yes, that is a generalization, but it illustrates the point. Whatever you pour into your subconscious mind becomes part of your programming, so choose wisely.

Some Examples of Pure Affirmations

I always have more money than I need.

I am lucky. I am blessed. I expect and get miracles.

I am so happy to be financially independent and free.

My beliefs match my Goals and Visions.

I can easily afford to own and maintain any home I choose to buy.

The beauty of where I live amazes me.

I love earning more than enough money to be self-employed.

It feels so good to be accepted into Florida State University.

I always read my Top 4 Goals and Top 4 Visions everyday.

I always easily complete my Top 4 Daily and Top 4 Weekly actions.

My Theory of Displacement

Pure Affirmations function through the Law of Attraction by the concept of *you get what you think and feel most often.* I have come up with a way of understanding this that I like to call my **Theory of Displacement**. This theory is best described with a clear phrase and a good analogy that explains exactly how the idea works.

First, the phrase:

"Fill your mind up with the things that you want, until they overflow all of the things you don't."

Then the analogy:

Imagine that you have a stockpot of dingy water in your sink. If you simply turn the water on, even at a slow streaming pace, and allow clean water to flow into the pot, very quickly, the clean water will *displace* the dingy water and the entire stockpot will be filled with clear water. You will not have to pour any old water out, yet the pot will hold new, crystal clear water in a matter of minutes.

In a way, this is exactly how Pure Affirmations operate and clear your mind. They will displace any limiting beliefs with the slow, steady filling up of new, clear ideas. In fact, I would not waste any time trying to figure out what your old, limiting beliefs are. Just use my *Theory of Displacement* to pour more of what you *do* want into your mind (with your Pure Affirmations) until those ideas and feelings wash away any previous concepts of lack or limitation.*

(*I am not a psychiatrist and this book is not intended to diagnose or treat any serious phobia or ailment.)

***

Now it's time to do your Chapter 4 Assignment. Consider your Top 4 Goals and Top 4 Visions. Also remember your Main Mission. Think about how their completion will look, feel and be described in the now. Write several Pure Affirmations of your own based on these intentions (at least one for each of your Top 4 Goals and Top 4 Visions, but there is really no limit). Also add a few things you are actively grateful for, like your health, fitness, clear mind or imagination. Record them in your preferred method. You will add to them and refine them as you continue along your path, but for now get them started.

Your Pure Affirmations will become a valuable component to your *Espresso For Your Goals* system. They will serve to help you fill your subconscious mind with more of what you want so that you deliberately fuel the Law of Attraction in ways that are to your highest benefit. Create your set of Pure Affirmations before moving ahead.

So far we have spent time assembling the parts of your system. The next chapter, Refocus Affirmations, is the last of these components. The section after that is when we finally see the espresso come together in the cup. The GVA Process will let you take each of these ingredients and align them with your daily actions in a simple, delicious way that is concentrated, effective and fun. Trust your barista, and meet me in Chapter 5.

CHAPTER 5

Refocus Affirmations

Refocus Affirmations differ from Pure Affirmations in both their structure and intent. Where Pure Affirmations (that you just created in the last chapter) are structured as ideal desired results, Refocus Affirmations are brief statements that illustrate things and events that are already completely true for you.

As such, the intent of Pure Affirmations is not to reprogram your subconscious, but rather to change your current vibration (or emotional state and feeling) so that you can function on that level and thereby attract equal energies.

Refocus Affirmations are most useful to help you refocus in times of contrast (hence the name). For instance, if you are still working in a job that you are striving to move beyond, and the worst of the reasons why has overwhelmed you on a particular day, then you would read your Refocus Affirmations the second you get off, in order to *refocus* your energy to align with your goals (what you do want) and not bemoan all night what you don't (your current job's issues).

This is why it is important that your Refocus Affirmations be about things that are true and indisputable. Times of serious contrast are not the times for dreamy visions of what may come.

In short, Refocus Affirmations are concise, true phrases that describe or conjure feelings or memories that resonate at the same frequency of what you are trying to achieve. This is most definitely advanced goal setting strategy, and at first glance the concept may seem complex, but the illustration below makes the idea clear.

For example, let's say you want a promotion that you have applied for, but you have not heard from your Regional Manager (or whomever makes that decision) yet. However, you *did* get a promotion into the position you have *now* and the new promotion would be the ideal next step for you as a leader. Yet every day you work with the other worthy candidates and wonder when you will all learn who got the job; the suspense is killing you.

Your Refocus Affirmations might say:

"I loved hearing my last boss tell me I got the promotion into this position I have now!"

"I love celebrating a promotion by going out to dinner with my family and friends. We had so much fun last time!"

"It feels so good knowing that I earned my promotion! I deserved it and I nailed it."

All of those statements would be one hundred percent true for you if you were promoted in the past. And they would absolutely help offer the vibration or feelings of being successfully promoted as you await the news of your recently applied for next promotion. Do you see the power of Pure Affirmations in times of contrast?

The phrase *"I got the new promotion! It's a done deal,"* (before you actually have) is great content for a Pure Affirmation that you created at the end of the last chapter (to be glanced at quickly without consciously judging the statement). But when you are realizing in vivid detail that you have not achieved something yet, create a Refocus Affirmation of something that is true and that has a similar or identical feeling, to consciously redirect your energy.

Another example is from my own personal experience. While still striving to become a completely self-employed writer, I did have a few published, paid writing jobs under my belt. Anytime that my current situation pushed me into severe contrast (like being forced to work long, stressful, physically aching, mentally exhausting hours on something that was decidedly not writing or speaking) I would use the following Refocus Affirmations:

"I love making money from writing!"

"I love seeing my work published!"

"I love knowing people enjoy reading the things I have written!"

"I absolutely love the excitement of seeing money deposited into my account, as I earn thousands of dollars from writing!"

All of those things were already true for me at the time, and they helped me to redirect my energy. Focusing on those true feelings kept me from complaining about the current jobs I had to do in the mean time, and helped me to move ahead to the day of having more than enough writing and speaking income to truly do what I love to do full time. Sweet!

So Refocus Affirmations are:

* Short statements *that are true* for you *now*.

* Used to deliberately refocus your vibrational offering by conjuring feelings similar to or identical to what you do want.

* Read consciously because they are facts, and as such, are used to help you focus on what success feels like in the same area.

* Powerful, advanced tools used in times of extreme contrast (when the opposite of your goal or vision is imposing itself upon you).

***

Of course, here is your Chapter 5 assignment. Think of your own current situation. Are there days that you must do more of something you would rather replace with items from your Top 4 Goals or Top 4 Visions?

Also, consider what you have accomplished in the past that gave you the same or similar feelings to the goals you are working toward now. Maybe you got your Bachelors degree and are now close to finishing your Masters program, and those final few projects are all that remain. Maybe you are striving to obtain financing for a new home, and you can recall the feelings of buying your first townhouse and closing that deal. (Get the idea?)

Craft a few of your own Refocus Affirmations and record them in the same format that you have been using for the other components. Once you have them ready, gather everything we have made so far. This is an exciting time of convergence. In the next chapter you will learn about the GVA Process, where we will use each of the parts that we now have to methodically drive our accomplishments to the next level.

The components that we have created so far were designed to be clear, potent and no-nonsense. I hope you find them to be just that, and together we will align them using the GVA Process, decorate them with a few more details in the chapters beyond, and thereby create the concentrated energy boost of high achievement that the title of this book promises. If you have made it this far, then I know you are ready to get down to business, so we can move on to the business of getting down! Meet me in Chapter 6!

Chapter 6

The GVA Process

Just writing down your goals puts you into 10% of the population who do so, and reading them every day puts you in the even more elite company of a scant 5% (according to Ken Cheo in his article, *"Goal Setting: Why 90% Of Us Don't Do It Correctly"* published in the Boston Business Journal, September 11, 2012).

Now imagine how small of a group you join by writing down a Main Mission, Top 4 Goals, Top 4 Visions, Pure Affirmations to support them, and Refocus Affirmations to realign your energy as you go. The GVA Process will put you into an even more exclusive group of achievers by providing a routine for fueling your day with gratefulness, reading your intentions and affirmations each day, then driving toward them with concrete actions. The GVA Process is a simple but highly effective daily practice that has helped me achieve some of my most life transforming intentions. Do not underestimate the power of doing this every day.

GVA stands for *Gratitude, Vision* and *Action*. The GVA process consists of a single, hand written page divided into three sections. A section where you list what you are grateful for, a section where you review your visions (and goals) and a section where you outline your top 4 daily actions, and top 4 weekly actions. You write this page each day, either in the morning for the day, or the night before for the day ahead. As such, the top line should be a heading of sorts, such as a single line with the day, date, time, and the designation: GVA.

Then title the first section "Gratitude List". Under this section list five to ten things you are currently grateful for. As you write them, conjure the pure feelings of gratefulness for each one. Each one should be relatively brief. You know the details, so a short description should be enough to help you generate the feelings of gratitude associated with each. Ten things you are grateful for should take up about ten lines on a page, but there is no hard and fast rule. The important part is listing and feeling current gratitude. Gratefulness and complaint cannot reside in the same moment. As high achievers, we know that *like attracts like.* Listing and feeling gratitude generates the energy that will draw more things to be grateful for into your experience. Doing this daily builds a valuable momentum.

The next section of your GVA Page is entitled "Vision Review". Under this section, list each of the following notes (really write these words down): Main Mission, Top 4 Goals, Top 4 Visions, Pure Affirmations, Refocus as needed, Visualize Top 4's / 5 min ea. At some point in your day, read your Main Mission, Top 4 Goals and Visions, glance rapidly through your Pure Affirmations, and carry your Refocus Affirmations with you and refer to them if you experience severe contrast, and spend time clearly visualizing** each of your Top 4 Goals and Top 4 Visions.

As you do each of these things, check the notes off in this Vision Review section. (I make small boxes next to each one and check them off throughout the day, or at the day's end.) In this section I also include some extra things that I feel will help me move ahead. For instance, I might include a note to read whatever current self-improvement or productivity book I am working on at the time. I may also list watching the videos of one or two of my motivational heroes online. Also, I will include a note to meditate for 15 minutes.

***

**Visualizing is such a hotly discussed topic in the LOA community that I have to give you my next-level advice on the subject, so here it is. When visualizing, imagine yourself in scenarios where your ideal desired results are already completed. Do not imagine them to be in the future, but visualize them as if they are part of your crystal clear powerful now. Pretend in your mind that you are living those realities right now, and consider how doing so *feels*. Congratulate yourself for these outstanding accomplishments. Say things out loud like *"Thank God I pushed through and got to this point where I am absolutely working as a writer full time." "I knew I could do it!" "Hell yes! How good does this feel, to be going to Napa Valley for a month!"* Imagine that you are talking to a friend about the goal you have accomplished. Laugh out loud at your amazing success in the areas of your goals. It only takes five minutes each or so. You will know when you capture the right feeling and have felt it enough, then move on. Pull that off for each of your highest goals and visions for five minutes each day, then email me in a few months to let me know how blown away you are.

***

Now all of this may seem like it would take up a large amount of time, but reading all of your Main Mission, Top 4's, Pure Affirmations, and visualizing each Goal and Vision for five minutes each only takes a total of about 45 minutes. Meditate for 15 minutes and you are at an hour. I usually spend about 20 minutes writing out my GVA

Process each day. So now we are at ninety minutes, which is the average length of a movie. And this is not ninety minutes in a row. Once you have your Vision Review section written, you have a whole day to get each thing done. It's easy and so worth it. Particularly for us high achievers in the top, dare I say now, one or two percent who would go to such concentrated efforts. Consider how many people do absolutely nothing toward their "goals" or wishes. How many hours does the average person squander playing games on their phone or watching some TV show?

I'm sure that if you are at this stage in this book you are the type of achiever who already spends an hour or so each day working on your goals and intentions. The reason for the *Espresso For Your Goals* system is not to give you more to do, but to streamline what you already do and add some methodical process to your accomplishment activity.

The next section of the GVA Process is the Action Section. The first heading for this section is entitled "Top 4 Actions Today". Under it, list the top 4 actions that you can take today that would move you closer to your Top 4 Goals or Top 4 Visions. You don't have to have an action for each of your Top 4 Goals, although you might. Sometimes you may have 4 actions that are all focused on one of your Top 4 Goals or Visions, and other times you may have a few from each. The important part is to choose actions of highest impact, and necessity. For example, when creating this book, I had an action to order the artwork. This became a priority, because I needed the artwork before I could order the video trailer, which was on my "Top 4 Actions This Week" list, which is the next and final heading for the GVA Process.

The "Top 4 Actions This Week" heading is exactly that. It concludes the Action section. I like to list the top 4 actions I need to complete before Sunday, midnight each week, rather that having a rolling seven days.

It is important to limit your actions to four per day, and four per week. You may have other, longer lists for yourself, but these are actions focused directly on the Top 4 Goals and Top 4 Visions you are working on at the moment. Four things get done; twenty things do not. This is not your all inclusive to-do list for your day and week; it is only your actions that are in alignment with accomplishing your highest intentions. Check them off as you do each one.

These Actions are tasks that you have complete control over doing. In other words, these actions are not more goals that would be nice to get done (like meeting a new person to date). Sometimes these actions may be massive (like finalizing a real estate contract). Other times they may be simple (like working on a certain presentation for at least thirty minutes today). If you commit to doing this GVA Process each and every day, you will be amazed at what you will accomplish.

Up until now I have said to create your components in whatever form works for you. For Main Mission, Goals, Visions and Affirmations you know I like 3x5 index cards, but you may swear by your computer notes, tablet *stickies*, yellow sticky notes in your notebook, or notes on your smartphone. I still think index cards rule, but whatever works for you. However, when it comes to the GVA Process, it should indeed be hand written. A spiral bound, college ruled notebook works perfectly. Some may prefer a legal pad. Either way, such notebooks or pads keep you on point when it comes to doing something like this that requires one page per day, no fail. (This would be part of that *"stick to the system the way it is the first time around"* bit.) I am on my fifth GVA spiral notebook. Looking back through them can generate a powerful feeling of accomplishment and dedication in and of itself, as well as being a reminder of how far you have come and how many things you have accomplished along the way.

Your GVA Pages will grow to look very similar each day. You will have the Gratitude List section at the top, listing five to ten things you are grateful for. Under that you will have your Vision Review section with check boxes next to the things you will do that day to read and focus on your goals, visions, and personal growth. Then below that you will have your Action section listing the Top 4 Actions Today, then Top 4 Actions This Week. You may modify a few details but stick to the general concept. From now on you will create this GVA Process page **every day**. You will grow to love it. Make your first one tonight if you are the *"do it before bed for the next day"* type, or begin fresh tomorrow morning if you are a *"program your day in the morning"* type (like me).

Tying The System Together

So now you have the basic *Espresso For Your Goals* system in place. Here is the summary of how it works.

Every day do the GVA Process by hand writing your GVA page beginning with your Gratitude List (and re-member to feel true gratefulness for each thing as you write it down).

Then, in the Vision Review section, list the phrases *Main Mission, Top 4 Goals, Top 4 Visions, Pure Affirmations, Refocus Affirmations, Visualize Top 4's – 5 min ea.*, and add any motivational reading or videos, and the like.

As you go through your day, check these components off as you read or do them. So for instance, once you read your Top 4 Goals on that day, you check that note off in the Vision Review section, and so on.

Next (in the Action Section) list the Top 4 Actions you can take today, and the Top 4 Actions you can take this week. These actions are tasks that are completely in your control, and that you believe will have the highest impact on accomplishing any, some, or all of your current Top 4 Goals and Visions. Now is the time to make these steps Specific, Measureable, Achievable, Realistic, and Time-Sensitive (as we discussed in the Top 4 Goals chapter).

As you complete each Action, check them off on your GVA Process page. If you do not get everything done, move them to the next day, or replace in whatever way moves you forward. Have fun with this process. One of my Pure Affirmation cards actually reads,

"I always complete my Top 4 Daily and Top 4 weekly Actions easily and smoothly in the most enjoyable ways," because I felt like I could do a better job of getting each done, but no one is judging you. This is *your* system. The idea is to chart your intentions and move toward them with action.

The *Espresso For Your Goals* system is all about aligning the powerful tools of written goals with the undeniable necessity of clear action. Remember, these actions are the natural, obvious next steps along your path of accomplishment. If it feels forced, rethink it. These actions should flow from your ideal desired result, not force and push toward it. Work this system for a month and see how you like it. At that time you might have some adjustments or changes to make it better for yourself. You can always visit espressoforyourgoals.com to give me feedback or let me know your success stories or ideas to improve the system.

Outstanding Job! You have completed and set into motion a deliberate, powerful system of being grateful for what you have, then writing down, reading, affirming, refocusing, and taking action toward your highest goals and visions. If you were already an established deliberate creator who wrote down and consciously worked toward goals and dreams, you were in the top 10% of the population. Welcome to the next level, the fearless few. Welcome to the *Espresso For Your Goals* Fellowship.

***

The next three chapters consist of The One Week Intention, Fast Forward Journaling and the Mentor Book. These three components are final touches to the *Espresso For Your Goals* system. They are the *half a raw sugar and a drop of cream* in the double espresso energy boost for our highest achievements to come. Each of these *decorations* will serve to propel your goals. Sometimes they may be a part of your GVA Process in the Vision Review section, or they may find their way into your Top 4 Actions Today or This Week. We are now beyond the pale. There is no going back. You know too much. See you in Chapter 7!

CHAPTER 7

The One Week Intention

As you progress along the path of accomplishing your Main Mission, Top 4 Goals and Top 4 Visions, you will naturally create daily and weekly actions that align with these goals. Part of what makes the GVA Process so effective, is its continuous nature. When using it, you are writing a daily Gratitude List, reading your mission and goals everyday, and creating your own list of actions to move you forward.

As you use this system you will accomplish some things with alarming speed, and others may take more time. I am often asked how long it will take for a certain goal to manifest in someone's life. My answer is: *how long will it take you to change your beliefs?*

How complete is your belief that you can and will accomplish something? If your belief is certainty, then you will recognize the full potential of your goal. Recognizing your goal's potential and being certain of its attainment allows you to take action. Actions toward your goal create results. These results, no matter how small or great, reinforce your beliefs and you spiral up to your achievement. This spiral will also work (quite rapidly) in reverse. If you are skeptical about accomplishing a goal, you fail to realize potential opportunities. This causes you to miss taking the correct actions and your results fail to match your hopes. This failure reinforces your original skepticism. This is a detailed description of the old axiom that the rich get richer and the poor get poorer. It is the basis for the idea that you get what you expect.

The complete truth is you get the results you expect, believe and take action toward, which leads to more results. This cycle cultivates more belief so you can then adjust your actions and progress with persistence until you arrive at your goal fulfilled.

The One Week Intention is a tool to help bring about a specific result, and it gains its power by alignment with your honest beliefs. This chapter explains how to implement The One Week Intention. First I will give you a summary of how the One Week Intention works, then I will give you an example to clearly describe the process so you can use it to add value to your own system.

Summary of The One Week Intention

Develop your One Week Intention by first choosing one of your Top 4 Goals or Top 4 Visions. Then consider a next logical component or accomplishment that would take you closer to achieving the goal you chose. Refine the details of that component and rate your personal believability that you will accomplish it in the week on a scale of 1 to 10 (with 1 being impossible and 10 being inevitable). Write it out in goal lingo, in the present and as if it were done.

The ideal component should have a believability of 8 or higher. Fine tune the wording or parts of the component until you reach that level 8 or more believability then release the thought of it and go about your week. Follow your intuitions and impulses and be alert to ways to get it done. If, at the end of the week you have accomplished the One Week Intention, replace it with the next logical step and repeat the process.

If you gain no ground on this particular One Week Intention, do not continue to pound on it week after week. Let it go and create another One Week Intention from a completely unrelated goal. Yes we must be persistent with our Main Mission and Top 4 Goals and Visions, but when it comes to this exercise the power of it comes from accomplishing an intended component.

A Hypothetical Example of The One Week Intention

In the area where I live in sunny Florida, we have a large number of seasonal residents who live here for the winter, then live up north in the summer. Rather than pay multiple service companies to maintain their home in their absence (such as a separate lawn service, pool keeper and pest control service) many people simply hire one Home Maintenance contractor who in turn manages those service vendors and becomes one point of contact for the homeowner. Let's say that you discovered this niche when you were managing the pool service company where you work now, and it is one of your Top 4 Goals to be a professional self-employed Home Maintenance contractor.

Perhaps you have even gotten one customer already and have set up the services and all is running fine. However, in order to confidently quit your day job and become truly self-employed doing this, you would need at least four more clients at the same rate of profit as the first. Your time is thin, your day job continually challenges your energy, but you know you can do this so you recommit and press on.

Brainstorm to come up with ideas for your One Week Intention. Initially your One Week Intention might be to find the next four customers and sign the contracts so that you can accomplish your goal of being 100% self employed. Write the goal out in the powerful present tense as if it were done. Then honestly and objectively rate your accomplishment believability from 1 to 10. You may think, *finding all four and signing contracts in a week would take a miracle actually. It's already Monday. I have XYZ to do on Tuesday. That only leaves three weekdays. I would rate that a 2.*

If you think the probability of actually accomplishing your first idea is about equal to the chances of dropping a cotton ball off of the Empire State Building and having it land on someone you know, then you need to refine.

So then you might cut it in half. What is your belief that you could find two more jobs like the first and sign contracts in the week? That might bring your belief up to a 5. It's possible, but still would be considered a stroke of luck if you did it. If so, reduce more. Finally you land on finding one new customer and contracting for the business. When you honestly examine your belief in accomplishing that intention you may be at a level 6 or 7.

Then drill down deeper into the language of your intention. What about it is keeping you from certainty? You want to arrive at a level 8 or above. In this example, simply removing the phrase *signing the contract* would probably do it. So your One Week Intention would be:

I have identified the perfect potential next customer and am set to meet with them to discuss the details. I know this will take me one step closer to my goal of self-employment. Rock on.

Then include that in your Pure Affirmations each day. Visualize it in the morning, visualize it at night and otherwise forget it.

***

Remember this is not selling out or watering down any of your Top 4 Goals or Top 4 Visions. You are simply refining a single component (a component that you would have to accomplish anyway) to a level of certainty. The power of the One Week Intention tool is that it allows you to experience the power of certainty.

Therefore, a key component to the tool is this: If you achieve the One Week Intention, outstanding. Create the next level for the next week and keep going.

If you *do not* gain any ground on it, put it away for a time. You can always come back to it and it will be turnkey and ready to go. Choose another Top 4 Goal and make a totally different One Week Intention for the next week. (Such as a commitment to do your maximum number of sit-ups every other day to accomplish your goal of having a flat stomach.)

The One Week Intention is a powerful tool in your goal achieving arsenal. Once you use it successfully you will be able to build momentum on something specific each week. I know you will use this to great success and I can't wait to hear about your experiences with it.

***

The next chapter gives you one of my favorite methods for achieving results. I call it Fast Forward Journaling. If you like detail and deep visualization this is your chance. Doing it is not only easy and fun, but is exceedingly effective. You may think you know what it's all about from the title, and you may be exactly right. In fact you may have heard of something similar or done something like it on your own. For me it was one of those ideas that when I first considered it, I just knew it would be powerful. I was right. Find your favorite cool pen and some paper and meet me in Chapter 8.

Fast Forward Journaling

The benefit of this goal accomplishment tool is in its multilayered nature. It can help you achieve powerful results because it works on many levels at once. Once you understand how to do it, it almost becomes second nature and therefore I will give you the gift of time by not going into any unnecessary details about how to apply the tool.

Suffice it to say that it is easy, fun and it has the potential to become one of those processes in your goal setting life that you will look back on with fondness, and look forward to with excitement. In this chapter I will define exactly what Fast Forward Journaling is and what makes it so powerful.

***

Fast Forward Journaling is a process that uses the power of *acting as if your goal is achieved* to help you give thoughts and energy to your ideal desired result. The more thought and emotion you give to the feeling of your ideal desired result, the more you fuel the Law Of Attraction. We know how tricky this can be, because it is very easy to give more thought to your goal being a reality sometime in the future, thereby perpetuating that *not there yet* state.

The Fast Forward Journaling tool allows you to completely bypass the *not yet* state mentally, and feel the finished goal's emotions. It is powerful because it is handwritten, comes from the perspective of completion, and is something that many people already do (journaling about reality that is).

You can use a page here and there in your normal journal notebook if you use one, or you can designate a notebook specifically for Fast Forward Journaling.

The process is easy and fun. Simply write out a single page in your journal from the perspective of a day when your goal is done and living. Let your self flow and write from the heart. Pretend you are in the future and this is really your journal entry for whatever is happening in your life. Rejoice. Remember. Complain. Plan. Reflect. There is no right or wrong thing to say, as long as you write as if your goal or goals are achieved and active in your experience.

For instance, you may write about the meeting you had with your real estate customer and how glad you are that the closing went well. You could write about being excited that your reservation and deposit are in order to rent the house in Napa Valley for your vacation (and that you can't wait to tell your family when you see them). Or you could write an entry about how concerned you are that your online T-shirt sales may outpace your manufacturing timeline.

So you get the idea. Remember it only needs to be a page or so, and you can do it as often as you like. Sometimes I go for stretches where I write in my Fast Forward Journal everyday. Other times I will leave it out of my routine for a while. There is really no hard and fast rule, but it does help build belief and as you do it you are using the hand written word and you can't help but visualize as you write. I also read pages back to myself periodically just to cultivate more thought around what I am working on.

Being a writer by nature, Fast Forward Journaling is one of my most treasured tools for accomplishing goals. I remember writing a Fast Forward Journal entry that described how thrilled I was to be meeting with the editor for a writing job. Some time later I had this strange sense of déjà vu as I was writing in my actual journal about a meeting with the editor of a newspaper I was writing an article for. I dug back through my Fast Forward Journal and found that page and all I could say was *Wow*. Little moments like that give us faith and hope and help us move on to greater things in our deliberate creation activities.

I hope you have some fun successes with Fast Forward Journaling and I would love to hear about them. Remember, you are always welcome to email me from our website at espressoforyourgoals.com

***

Outstanding! This is the last content chapter in Espresso For Your Goals. Congratulations on your persistence and commitment to finish the book and I hope you will use the system to your greatest success. The final chapter that follows is simply a summary of the material and will serve as your last sip of espresso. I hope you are fully energized by it and the entire system. On to the summary and thank you for your time and attention.

CHAPTER 9

Summary and Conclusion

As I write this final summary I am realizing the fact that I have very nearly accomplished one of my most desired goals. I began working on the Espresso For Your Goals project on October 10, 2013. Today is December 19, 2013 and what an outstanding gift I am giving myself this Yule Season just two days before the Winter Solstice which is not only the longest night of the year, but my father's birthday as well. I have to believe that such convergent moments are powerful and auspicious in the best way.

I have learned a few things about myself along the way and I hope you have learned some valuable things about yourself as well.

If you are reading this page and have applied the steps and methods in this system then you and I have a few things in common. We never give up. We thrive on solid, undisputed accomplishment. We consume and bestow genuine compliments with abundant enthusiasm. We fully and deeply believe that we deserve the achievement of all of our highest goals and visions. And we are confident that we now have the tools to systematically fuel our top desires with powerful language, gratitude, actions and results.

Consider how many people never do a single thing to achieve a single goal. Maybe you know someone who is intelligent and hard working, but convinced that the power to do something profound is out of their control. If so, share Espresso For Your Goals with them by giving it as a gift. Or send them to Amazon.com to buy this book in paperback like you are reading now, in eBook format for Kindle (or any eBook reader) or just let them borrow your copy. Who knows how many people we can help together.

Remember to push on no matter what. Write your GVA Page everyday. What is important in the Action section is not what you write, but what you do. Put yourself in that top elite few who plan their life and live their plan. Will everything work out exactly as you imagine? No. But the adventure is in the road trip to your goals and the accomplishments that do work out perfectly are the jewels that we find along the way.

As you accomplish your Top 4 Goals and Visions, remind yourself of how you did it. Record your successes, so you can move on to your highest dreams with the certainty that big intentions demand. In ten weeks I used this system to conceive, outline, plan, write and publish the book and system that you now hold in your hand and mind. What can you do in ten weeks? I would love to hear about your goals and successes. Please share them with me and stay in touch!

I would be so grateful if you would please leave your honest review of this work for the benefit of other potential readers.

I wish you the most outstanding success for the highest good of all. Best wishes and I will talk to you soon.

—*Les Goodrich*

Exciting Video Course Offer

If you would like to supercharge your system further, in more detail and through the magic of our **Espresso For Your Goals Video Course**, simply follow the link below espressoforyourgoals.com/video-course-member-access to gain access to the Video Course Members Area. Yes it is something I am selling, but it's a serious value, and it's really cool too.

Here is what you will find inside:

*A series of **FIVE Video Modules** where each topic in the *Espresso For Your Goals System* is *coached in detail* with *examples* and *easy-to-follow instructions* and *Tips!*

***A Printable Workbook** designed specifically for use in conjunction with the Video Modules.

***Pure Affirmations MP3**: An Audio Recording of Pure Affirmations that is exceedingly motivational and powerful, with tips for leveraging this tool for an even greater impact.

***FREE BONUS #1:** The *"To Manifest Abundant Wealth"* Mind Movie Video I created for myself, and now you can use it too.

FREE BONUS #2:** The Mentor Book process revealed! This is a powerful motivational tool that I invented and have never shared with anyone before. This one tool has helped me out of some sticky situations, and it is yours free, as my way of saying ***thank you when you purchase the **Espresso For Your Goals Video Course!**

I could easily sell the video modules and workbook alone for about $50 on clickbank (and someday I might). So why don't I, you ask? Because for now I am more interested in writing than Internet Marketing. Besides, I created this course to offer **even more depth** and **result-generating value** *for you*, the person cool enough and persistent enough to buy, read and use my book. When I priced the <u>**Espresso For Your Goals Video Course**</u> offer, my goal was to create a video course with enough value and free bonuses to be worth easily ***triple the price*** I would sell it for. I fully believe that I have met or exceeded that goal.

This powerful and fun <u>**Espresso For Your Goals Video Course**</u> is available for <u>**one single payment**</u> of <u>**only $27.**</u> **(This price is subject to change and will likely increase with subsequent updates of this book and the video course itself. However, if you find the video course price on the link page is higher than the price shown above, simply email us your purchase receipt with date and we will honor the lowest price. Thank you.)**

Now I put a lot more work into it than that, because that is just kind of the way I am (as you may have figured out by now). Think about it: how do you feel about the content and value in this book, compared to the price you spent to get it? So as a result of my overachiever personality, you are assured to get much more value out of the video course than the small, more than fair price of $27. But even so, it still comes with my <u>solid money-back guarantee</u>.**

** My _solid money-back guarantee_ is this: If you are not completely satisfied with the **Espresso For Your Goals Video Course** product once you have purchased it and genuinely tried it, just let me know and I will refund your money 100%, no questions asked.
–Les Goodrich.

So just *visit the web address below* to get the **Espresso For Your Goals Video Course**, and I will see you inside the course Members Area. Rock On!

espressoforyourgoals.com/video-course-member-access

www.ingramcontent.com/pod-product-compliance
Lightning Source LLC
Chambersburg PA
CBHW021220020426
42331CB00003B/402